GETTING TO KNOW THE WORLD'S GREATEST ARTISTS

P A U L
KLEE

WRITTEN AND ILLUSTRATED BY MIKE VENEZIA

CONSULTANT MEG MOSS

CHILDRENS PRESS®

CHICAGO

Cover: *Around the Fish.* 1926. Oil on canvas, 18⅜ x 25⅛ inches.
Collection, The Museum of Modern Art, New York.
Abby Aldrich Rockefeller Fund.
Photograph © 1991 The Museum of Modern Art, New York.
© 1991, ARS, NY/Cosmopress, Geneva

For Debbie

Library of Congress Cataloging-in-Publication Data

Venezia, Mike.
   Paul Klee / by Mike Venezia.
          p.   cm. — (Getting to know the world's greatest
artists)
   Summary: Discusses, in simple text, the life and work of
the abstract painter, focusing on his use of color, shape,
and symbolism.
   ISBN 0-516-02294-6
   1. Klee, Paul, 1879-1940—Criticism and
interpretation—Juvenile literature.   [1. Klee, Paul, 1879-
1940. 2. Artists. 3. Painting, German. 4. Painting,
Modern—Germany. 5. Art appreciation.] I. Title.
II. Series.
ND588.K5V46   1991
759.9494—dc20   91-12554
[B]   CIP
                                                         AC

Lost in Thought. 1919. Pencil on notepaper, mounted on board,
10⅝ x 7¾ inches. The Blue Four-Galka Scheyer Collection. Norton
Simon Museum, Pasadena. © 1991, ARS, NY/Cosmopress, Geneva

Paul Klee (pronounced "klay")
was born near Bern, Switzerland, in
1879. He was an important artist and
a very good musician, writer, and
teacher. He used all his talents to make
a remarkable kind of modern art.

Paul Klee loved color. Most of his paintings and other works of art are filled with beautiful and exciting colors.

Sometimes you can recognize certain things in Paul Klee's paintings, such as people, animals, and houses. He also used numbers and letters of the alphabet as symbols that had a special meaning to him.

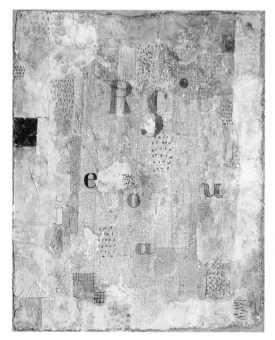

Vocal Fabric of the Singer Rosa Silber.
1922. Watercolor and plaster on
muslin, mounted on cardboard,
24½ x 20½ inches. Collection,
The Museum of Modern Art, New York.
Gift of Mr. and Mrs. Stanley Resor.
© 1991, ARS, NY/Cosmopress, Geneva

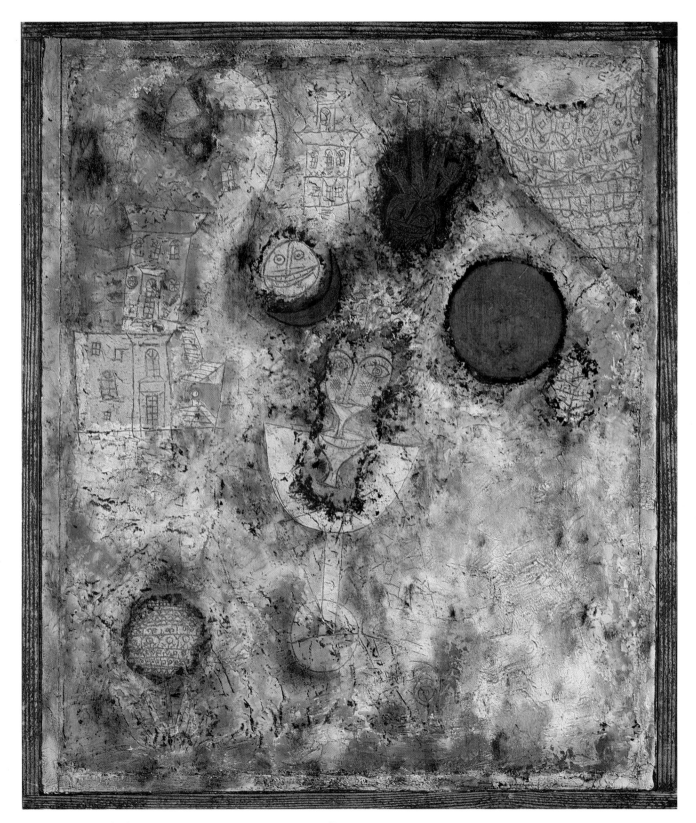

Magic Garden. 1926. Oil on plaster-filled wire mesh, 20⅞ x 17¾ inches.
Peggy Guggenheim Collection, Venice, The Solomon R. Guggenheim Foundation, New York.
Photograph by David Heald, © The Solomon R. Guggenheim Foundation.
© 1991, ARS, NY/Cosmopress, Geneva

Paul Klee's art is known as abstract art. The objects and figures in abstract art look different from the way they look in real life.

Sometimes the objects in an abstract painting don't look like anything at all.

Many of Paul Klee's greatest paintings are just colors and shapes.

Fire at Evening. 1929. Oil on cardboard, 13⅜ x 13¼ inches.
Collection, The Museum of Modern Art, New York.
Mr. and Mrs. Joachim Jean Aberbach Fund. © 1991, ARS, NY/Cosmopress, Geneva

Paul Klee always loved to draw.
When he was little he would visit
his Uncle Ernst's restaurant. Paul
imagined all kinds of interesting

things in the patterns of the marble tabletops there. He traced what he saw onto paper.

Paul Klee grew up in a very musical family. His mother was a singer and his father was a music teacher. They taught Paul to play the violin quite well when he was very young.

Both music and art were important
to Paul. It took him a long time to
decide whether to become an artist or
a musician.

Finally Paul decided to study art in the city of Munich, Germany. Munich was an important art center at the beginning of the 20th century — artists there were trying new and exciting things.

Paul met some of those artists, and soon became friends with them. Wassily Kandinsky, Franz Marc, and August Macke painted in a new style that Paul had never seen before.

Lady in a Green Jacket. 1913.
By August Macke, oil on canvas,
17½ x 17⅛ inches.
Wallraf-Richartz Museum,
Cologne. SuperStock, NY

Blue Mountain. 1908-1909. By Wassily Kandinsky,
oil on canvas, 41¾ x 38 inches,
gift of Solomon R. Guggenheim, 1941.
Solomon R. Guggenheim Museum,
New York. Photograph by David Heald,
© The Solomon R. Guggenheim Foundation.
© 1991, ARS, NY/ADAGP

Yellow Cow. 1911. By Franz Marc, oil on canvas, 55⅜ x 74½
inches. Solomon R. Guggenheim Museum, New York. Photograph by David
Heald, © The Solomon R. Guggenheim Foundation

Paul liked the bright colors and shapes these artists used, and the simple, almost childlike way they painted people and objects.

He realized that a painting didn't have to look like a photograph to be a good painting.

Paul worked very hard to learn all that he could about drawing with line.

Caricature of a young woman in simple contour, 1908. Pencil on paper, 4¹/₁₀ x 4 inches. Paul Klee Foundation, Museum of Fine Arts, Bern. © 1991, ARS, NY/Cosmopress, Geneva

Comedian. 1904. Etching and aquatint, printed in black, plate, 6¹/₁₆ x 6⅝ inches. Collection, The Museum of Modern Art, New York. Purchase Fund. © 1991, ARS, NY/Cosmopress, Geneva

Then he learned how to give things shape and how to make things seem solid.

Finally he learned about color.

Paul also traveled as much as he could to see and learn from the works of the world's great artists.

Detail of *Senecio* on page 28

18

It was on one of his trips that Paul Klee decided he would spend the rest of his life as an artist. While he was visiting Tunisia, Africa, Paul noticed how colorful things were in this beautiful and mysterious country. He thought the light there gave everything a fairytale look. Paul Klee couldn't wait to start painting what he saw.

The next day Paul began painting watercolors of Tunisia. Paul showed the excitement he felt during his trip by changing the natural shapes and colors of things.

Detail of *Kairouan*. 1914.
Watercolor mounted on cardboard,
$8^8/_{10}$ x $9^1/_{10}$ inches.
Donation of Kurt Fried, 1978.
Museum der Stadt, Ulmer Museum, Ulm.
Photograph © Bernd Kegler, © 1991,
ARS, NY/Cosmopress, Geneva

Paul Klee changed the natural look of things in his paintings for a reason.

Up until Paul Klee's time, artists painted what they liked to look at, or things they were familiar with. Paul and his friends thought that a painting should be more than that. Paul wanted his paintings to show worlds that had never been seen before.

Carnival in the Mountains. 1924.
Watercolor on paper, 10½ x 12 inches.
Paul Klee Foundation,
Museum of Fine Arts, Bern. © 1991,
ARS, NY/Cosmopress, Geneva

23

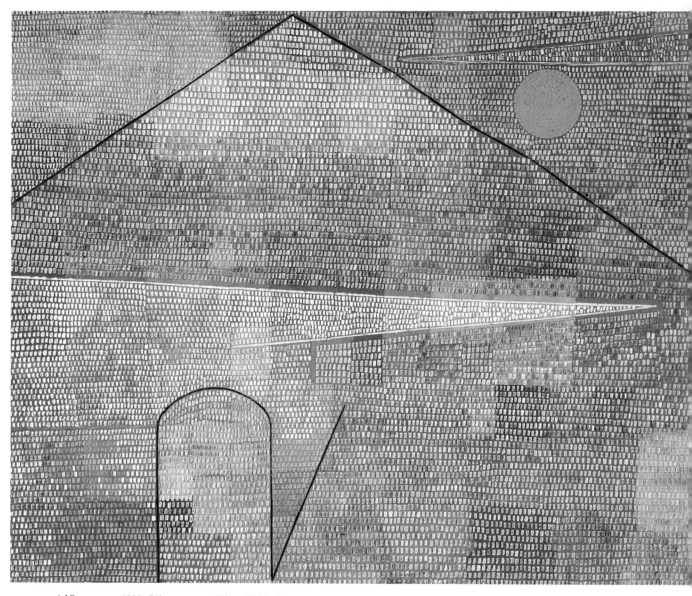

Ad Parnassum. 1932. Oil on canvas, 39½ x 49¼ inches.
Kunstmuseum, Bern. Bridgeman Art Library/SuperStock. © 1991, ARS,
NY/Cosmopress, Geneva

Paul thought it was important to
give the person looking at one of his
paintings (you) a special feeling
deep down inside. A feeling a person
couldn't get from an ordinary painting.

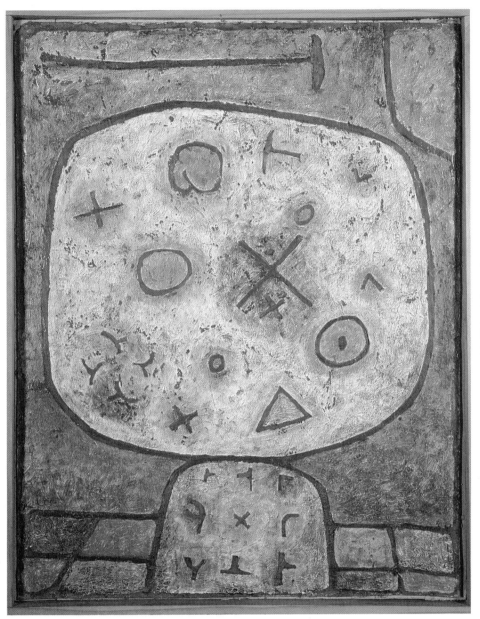

Flowers in Stone.
1939. Oil on cardboard,
19⅝ x 15⅝ inches.
Galerie Rosengart,
Lucerne. Bridgeman
Art Library/
SuperStock. © 1991,
ARS, NY/Cosmopress,
Geneva

If you look closely at a Paul Klee painting for a while, you might get a feeling of energy or movement through space, or see a microscopic world never seen before.

Paul gave some of his paintings
a musical feeling. Even though
paintings don't have sound, Paul's
patterns of color and shapes make many
people imagine the rhythm of music.

Fugue in Red. 1921.
Watercolor on paper,
9¾ x 14¾ inches.
Private Collection.
Bridgeman Art
Library/SuperStock.
© 1991, ARS,
NY/Cosmopress,
Geneva

Crystal Gradation. 1921. Watercolor, 9⅜ x 12⅝ inches.
Kunstmuseum, Basel. Photograph by Colorphoto Hans Hinz, Germany.
© 1991, ARS, NY/Cosmopress, Geneva

Senecio. 1922. Oil on canvas, 16 x 15 inches. Kunstmuseum,
Basel. Scala/Art Resource, NY. © 1991, ARS, NY/Cosmopress, Geneva

Paul Klee was always
experimenting with his painting
materials, and with the surfaces he
painted on. Sometimes he painted on
rough cloth with one kind of paint
and colored over it with another kind

Ab Ovo. 1917. Watercolor, 5¾ x 10¼ inches. Paul Klee Foundation,
Museum of Fine Arts, Bern. © 1991, ARS, NY/Cosmopress, Geneva

of paint. Paul used chalks, paste, and
even crayons to make colors seem like
they're glowing from inside. In some
of his works you can see the ragged
edges of the cloth or paper he painted on.

Paul Klee always felt close to nature and carefully studied the natural things around him.

Above: *Around the Fish*. 1926. Oil on canvas, 18⅜ x 25⅛ inches.
Collection, The Museum of Modern Art, New York.
Abby Aldrich Rockefeller Fund.
Photograph © 1991 The Museum of Modern Art, New York.
© 1991, ARS, NY/Cosmopress, Geneva

Room Perspective with Inhabitants.
1921. Watercolor, 19⅛ x 12½ inches.
Paul Klee Foundation,
Museum of Fine Arts, Bern.
© 1991, ARS, NY/Cosmopress, Geneva

When he was a teacher, Paul taught his students not to imitate a camera, which copies objects as they appear. He wanted his students to look below the surface of things — to find new and exciting worlds.

Paul Klee's paintings often show his sense of humor. Sometimes he used interesting titles to make his paintings more fun.

Right: *Twittering Machine.* 1922. Watercolor and pen and ink on oil transfer drawing on paper, mounted on cardboard, 25¼ x 19 inches. Collection, The Museum of Modern Art, New York. Purchase. © 1991, ARS, NY/Cosmopress, Geneva

Below: *Death and Fire.* 1940. Oil, 18⅛ x 17⅜ inches. Paul Klee Foundation, Museum of Fine Arts, Bern. © 1991, ARS, NY/Cosmopress, Geneva

Near the end of his life, Paul Klee's colors became a little darker and the titles of his works became more serious. But he still painted pictures filled with fantasy and magic.

It's fun to see a real Paul Klee painting and try to figure out what paints and materials he used to make his abstract works of art so special.

The paintings in this book are from the museums listed below. If none of these museums are close to you, maybe you can visit one when you are on vacation.

Galerie Rosengart, Lucerne, Switzerland
Kunsthalle, Hamburg, Germany
Kunstmuseum, Basel, Switzerland
Kunstmuseum, Museum of Fine Arts, Bern, Switzerland
Museum der Stadt, Ulm, Germany
The Museum of Modern Art, New York, New York
Norton Simon Museum, Pasadena, California
Solomon R. Guggenheim Museum, New York, New York
Wallraf-Richartz Museum, Cologne, Germany